Parenting in a Social Media World

Connecting a Disconnected Generation

Dan Ortiz

DO
PUBLISHING

Parenting in a Social Media World

Connecting a Disconnected Generation

© 2021 by Dan Ortiz

All rights reserved solely by the author. The author guarantees all contents are original and do not infringe upon the legal rights of any other person or work. No part of this book may be reproduced in any form without the permission of the author. The views expressed in this book are not necessarily those of the publisher.

Printed in the United States of America.

ISBN-13: 978-17359627-3-3

LCCN: 2021900362

DO PUBLISHING

Lakeland, Florida

Dedication

I want to dedicate this book to my beautiful wife and best friend, Jennifer Ortiz who has been by my side for the last 26 years. She is the biggest encourager you will ever meet. Our daughter Makenna who has pushed me to be a better father every day and has given me plenty of memories of our daily car rides while she was in High School. Tate Ortiz who encourages me in everything I do. Brycen Ortiz who just brings so much joy into our home and Morgan Ortiz who is the most loving kid you will ever meet.

I also want to dedicate this book to my mom and dad Angel and Leticia Ortiz who are no longer with us. Mom you taught me that God is good and He has our back no matter what the circumstance. It's a faith I carry with me on a daily basis. Dad you taught me that you can never go wrong by loving people and letting them know they are valued and important and to always smile and have a good time. I love you both dearly and miss you every day.

Acknowledgements

I don't know where to begin because there have been so many people that have blessed and influenced my life. You are only as strong as the people you have around you and I have been blessed to have had great people by my side.

First, I'd like to thank my sister Marely and her family who've always had my back in prayer and encouragement. I will always be thankful for her continuing my mom's legacy of prayer for our family. My brother Rey who has provided much needed wisdom in critical times in my life. My brother Angel who without his help I would not have been able to attend college.

My fraternity brother David Austin who introduced me to Peter Lopez. Peter, my brother, from the first time we spoke, I felt an immediate connection. Thank you for your encouragement and help publishing my first book. Nicole Donoho, although I know she probably wanted to strangle me several times during this process because I am not the best at keeping timelines, gently kept pushing me and encouraging me to get this book finished.

David and Amy Rhinehart who are family but also some of our dearest friends. Jen and I look forward to our Tuesday evening hangout night every week. David there are only a handful of people in this world that I know I can trust to have my back and also trust enough to tell me the truth. Thank you for always being there for me and I look forward to many more lunches at Winners. To one of my best friends in this world Marcus Stern who has been there for me for the last 14 years no matter what in the good times and the challenging times you are always by my side I appreciate you bro.

To my fraternity brothers in my inner circle Albert Laboy, Jon Potter, Sean McCall, David Austin, Ric Gill. I appreciate all of you more than you will ever know.

Attorney Edward Reyes, thank you for taking time out of your busy schedule to contribute to this book. I was honored to be able to attend your swearing in as an attorney and have enjoyed seeing you continue to grow your law practice by helping people. Your hustle is something I have respected from day one but more importantly your friendship is something I will always cherish. You can find Attorney Edward Reyes on Facebook at facebook.com/reyesoptions

Dr. Brian Beard I still remember meeting you as my RA at Lee University. You were one of the most welcoming and kind people that I meet in my first week there and you continue to be. Thank you for your contribution to this book. Even though we had not talked on the phone for years the power of Social Media has kept us connected all this time. I wish you continued success in your practice. You can find Dr. Beard on TicTok @drbrianccd

There are many more people that have impacted my life in a positive way I appreciate all of you. If I missed you, I sincerely apologize but know I am grateful for you.

Table of Contents

Dedication	ii
Acknowledgements	iv
Introduction	x
Social Doesn't Change You, It Reveals You	1
Don't Shoot the (Facebook) Messenger	11
Do You Want to be Right or Left (Disconnected)?	19
On-Stage vs. Backstage	27
It's Not the Devil, Mama	35
Navigating the Negative	53
Chillin' on the Back Porch	65
You've Got Mail	75
To Post or Not to Post?	81
Market Like a Gen Z	87
Above All Else, Just Get Connected	101
My Family's Quick Guide to Social Media Platforms	107

Introduction

Tweet. Post. Comment. Like. Retweet. Scroll. Swipe. Connect. Wait, are we actually connecting? Unless you live in a remote part of the world, or have your head in the sand, chances are you don't walk very far without seeing a cellphone. These devices and the apps they offer connect us to the world like never before. At least that's what the sales pitch's try to convince us. But, the reality is that they can also have a bad habit of disconnecting most of us from personal relationships, if we're not careful.

Social media doesn't seem to be slowing down anytime soon. There are those that see the disconnect and disfunction social media is causing in relationships. Some of them support throwing it out, while others embrace it to the extreme, posting minute-by-minute updates of their lives. How do we find balance and connection with people that are just a screen away? How do we make social media work for us rather than becoming a slave to the screen?

Throughout this book, that is exactly what I plan to discuss. We're going to talk about the good and the bad of this growing virtual world. And, just so it doesn't seem one-sided, I've recruited the help of my beautiful wife and four children to give their take on social media and the platforms being used. After each chapter, you'll find a **FAMILY CHAT** section, where I've included interviews from my family with their take on this virtual world.

Let's jump in and get started.

Chapter 1

Social Doesn't Change You, It Reveals You

Have you ever heard the scenario where a person comes into money and suddenly, they become a complete jerk? People say, "Oh they were such a nice guy until they came into money." The reality, in most cases, is that the person was a jerk before they ever had money. When they came into money it simply amplified their 'jerk' platform.

Social media works in a similar way. Everyone wants to push blame onto social media as the problem for people's disconnected and strained relationships. As the saying goes, "Guns don't kill people, people kill people." The same can be said here, "Social media doesn't disconnect people, people disconnect from other people."

Like a frying pan, a newspaper, a gun, a bottle of pills – social media is nothing more than a tool. In the right hands, it can be healthy and lifegiving. But in the wrong hands, it can turn destructive. People that want others to pity the hand they've been dealt will seek that kind of attention, whether it is in person or on social media. People who seek the praise of others will do so in a classroom, in a mall, on a sports field, or on a YouTube channel. People that think they are always right will say so, whether amongst friends, with a stranger at the store, or in the comment feed of a social media network.

Social media hasn't changed who we are. In reality, it has drawn back the curtain that once gave us personal space. In that way, social media has revealed who we are and often try to hide. With all the filters it often provides, it actually removed the "personal space" filter that most generations lived behind. The filter that kept people from sharing all their business and opinions. For some reason, you can take someone that is typically an introvert, hand them a social media app and suddenly they are sharing memes, commenting, and giving their opinions like they're a

'Chatty Cathy Doll.' Without the fear of looking the other person in the eye, we all seem to be a little braver than we normally would be.

This revelation about social media gave me a whole new perspective on myself and the tool I had been given. People are more likely to share stuff about themselves that they might not share in person, whether initially through a post or without thinking through a meme or video. They might be a very personal and private person but the fact that they liked or shared a meme talking about heartbreak shows me that they probably have experienced something along those lines. The fact they are sharing links about adoption shows me that could be a topic close to their heart. The list goes on and on.

So where did all this start anyway? Well, although it's not always the most accurate, Wikipedia has an interesting timeline[1] for social media. The

---

[1] https://en.wikipedia.org/wiki/Timeline_of_social_media

timeline starts in the 70's, which seems unbelievable since social media really didn't seem to become a widely used term until platforms like Myspace and Facebook emerged in 2003–04. Hard to imagine that 17 years ago we were just beginning to communicate via these social platforms. Now there are generations that have grown up knowing them as every day staples. There are generations that don't know what the world looked like without social media.

I remember when Myspace first came out. Yes, I had a Myspace account and I'm probably dating myself by admitting to that. Myspace allowed me to connect with friends from high school and see where they ended up in life. It was a good way to reconnect but nothing too deep or personal for me. Find a person, see where they live now, see where they work now. It was basic information. A great way to reconnect after you hadn't seen a classmate for a long time.

Then Facebook came along. I viewed Facebook as a place to voice my opinions. Who wouldn't want to hear what I had to say on topics? I obviously knew a lot more than most people did, in my mind, and I was going to make sure they were educated to the fullest.

During the 2008 Presidential elections, I found myself in many debates with friends that stood on the opposite side of the political fence. One person I remember having the most heated debates with was an associate pastor at our church. He was my pastor; he should stand for the same things that I stood for. At least that's what I thought at the time. Our comment threads went back and forth, with both of us standing our ground and digging our feet in deep to our mouths! There was no love or understanding in these comment thread debates. His opinion was right to him, my opinion was right to me, and neither of us were going to back down. We could say whatever we wanted to each other from the other side of our screen and there was no remorse for 'being right.'

But something happened along the way that altered the relationship, or lack thereof, that we had. He was diagnosed with cancer. His diagnosis was one of those deals that hit you with a "not a lot of time left" reality slap to the face. Let's face it, we all secretly think maybe we'll live forever or at least to the point where we start wearing down. When something like this happens, it makes you think, "Dammit, I just lost all this time I thought I had with this person."

Despite how our comment threads may have looked, we weren't enemies, and far from it. I had so much respect for him in "real life." So, when all this started with his health, I began visiting him in person. The political differences didn't leave our conversations, rather they evolved. While talking in person, neither of us had the privilege of voicing our opinion, hitting enter, and walking away. Now we had to take time listening to the other man's reasoning for his views.

These conversations never changed my political viewpoints, nor did they change his. But they did change each of our hearts. These in-person conversations allowed us to hear about how each other had grown up and why we landed on the political sides we did. I didn't agree with him but I was able to respect and have empathy for him. Now that I got to know him and why he believed the way he did, I no longer felt the need to stand my ground. I no longer wanted to change his mind or bring him to "my side." Instead, I learned to respect and accept our differences.

Eight to nine months after his diagnosis, he passed away. Looking back, it's sad to think I had wasted two years, allowing our differences to divide us, when I could have spent them building a stronger relationship with this man. We both had opinions, we both had platforms to voice them, and never once did we take time to recognize there was a live human with real emotions on the other side of the screen.

Leading up to his death, and especially after his death, I began looking at myself through the lens of my Facebook page. What did my social media account say about me? I have to admit, I didn't like what I saw. Facebook was my 'here's my opinion' platform and every comment revealed just how self-serving and arrogant I really was. There are many posts, where I look back and can't believe I posted such things.

Here I was thinking I was this nice guy and my Facebook timeline painted a much different picture of the man I was. That associate pastor wasn't the only person I had played "keyboard warrior" with either. As I stated earlier, my political "battles" touched many different people. I suppose I could go back and delete all those old posts, and erase all the evidence, like nothing ever happened. But the reality is that it did happen. It's a stark reminder of the man I was and never want to be again. I never want to forget that there's a person on the other side of the comment thread. A real live person, just on the other side of the screen, who may have different views from mine, but it doesn't make them wrong based on their upbringing and life experiences.

FAMILY CHAT

Now it's time for a quick chat with the family, to get their thoughts on social media. I'd like to take a moment to introduce you to my wife, Jennifer Ortiz, my daughter, Makenna (23), and my three sons – Tate (21), Brycen (18), and Morgan (12). Let see what they have to say…

Q- What are your thoughts on social media?

Jennifer Ortiz (my wife) – I think it has a purpose, if used properly. I think you can use it for positive. As far as for kids, I do think that it can be dangerous because they get a false sense of reality sometimes and they add a lot of pressure on themselves to be something. I have a love/hate relationship with it sometimes.

Morgan Ortiz (12) – I mainly just stay away from social media right now. I have no social media apps.

Brycen Ortiz (18) – It is something that, as I've gotten older, can be both good and bad. It can allow you to get connected with others and the bad is that it can have a lot of negative vibes.

Tate Ortiz (21) – I think it's great. But, there's a lot of bad things. Oversaturation of information a lot of times. It does help me stay connected with people though. I have friends in Connecticut that I never see and I'm able to stay connected with them via Snapchat.

Makenna Ortiz (23) – Social media is great, but it can also be really bad. There's so much negative that a person can get caught in but there is also so much potential to be creative and connect in new ways.

Chapter 2

Don't Shoot the (Facebook) Messenger

The revelation my Facebook timeline provided of who I really was meant it was time to shut down my accounts and be done with social media, right? That's what people are saying when they complain about kids spending way too much time on social media outlets, right? Nobody talks to each other anymore, people are no longer personal, and it's all the fault of technology, right?

Wrong! If the mailman delivers you a letter from your mother stating that you need to spend more time with your children, does getting a new mailman solve the issue? No. Does returning an angry letter to your mother about all her faults solve the issue? No. The only thing that solves the issue is evaluating yourself and excavating to the root of the problem. Are my priorities mixed up? Am I struggling with something that's isolating me from my family? Is my mother lashing out because she struggled as a parent and wants to make sure I don't make the same mistakes?

Okay, that last one is evaluating the messenger, rather than myself, but sometimes that is necessary as well. My point is that we need to get to the heart of the message and stop being so quick to shoot the messenger. (For the record, this mother scenario is a work of fiction and never happened in my life.)

In the 80's, teens stretched the 20-foot spiral cord to their bedroom, and spent hours behind their closed bedroom door, talking with their friends.

Men and women riding subways and buses buried their faces behind newspapers, rather than converse with other passengers.

Grandparents would recall the 'good ol' days,' as their grandchildren nodded, acknowledging that they were listening but unable to actually relate.

All these things were the way of life.

The 20-foot cord and closed bedroom doors were only the messengers of that day. They delivered a message crying out for independence and privacy saying, "I'm not a kid anymore and I'm trying to figure this out, so give me space."

The newspapers were messengers saying, "I'm not sure I want to know you or that I want you to know me. That's beyond my comfort zone."

And the nodding head was a reaction of respect. No child could really understand what was so good about walking to school *uphill* both ways. If I'm honest, I can't even understand why they were good ol' days.

In all cases, people typically attacked the messengers. Saying things such as:

"You're always on that phone."

"How come nobody ever talks on a bus? The media is to blame!"

"You act like you know but you don't know."

The messages are the same today, but the messengers have evolved.

Teens are still seeking their independence and privacy but the 20-foot cord has been replaced with mini computers they can carry anywhere.

Most people still aren't fans of stepping out of their comfort zones but their newspapers have been replaced with cellphones, laptops, and tablets.

Younger generations still struggle to understand and appreciate the 'wisdom' that older generations have gained through their hard times and struggles. But, sadly, the nodding heads have been mostly replaced with deep sighs or rolling eyes.

Similarly, to the 80's, we're still attacking the messengers, rather than decoding the messages. Now we find ourselves saying things such as:

"You're always texting people."

"That's all you ever do, look at your phone."

"You, young people, have no appreciation for what really matters in life."

As much as humans have advanced with our inventions and technology, our issues and struggles continue to remain the same. We continue to attack our kids, friends, family, and spouses, rather than address the heart of the issue. We should be asking ourselves questions such as:

- What is going on inside of me that is causing me not to talk to people at this luncheon?
- Why am I so insecure in a room full of people I don't know?

I see it happening all the time in professional circles. When someone is insecure, they turn to their phone and act like they are answering an email, text, etc. to avoid human interaction.

We are selfish, arrogant, and prideful; we now have platforms to ensure everyone knows we are right.

We are insecure, uncertain, and scared of rejection; we now have platforms to seek approval and praise.

We are all navigating through the uncertainties and unknowns of life; we now have platforms to make it look like we've found our way.

I'll say it again – social media is a tool. We have to decide how we are going to use it. So, how do we use it, rather than abuse it? How do we master it, rather than become its slave?

FAMILY CHAT

Q – What are the advantages or disadvantages of social media vs. phone calls?

Brycen Ortiz (18) – I think the advantage of Instagram, TikTok, and other sites is that you're able to bring positivity to peoples' lives – whether it is one single person or a group. However, with phone calls it's more of a one-on-one kind of relationship-building. When I call my brother in college and ask what he has been up to, I'm going to get more detailed information on a phone call than I would via social media. Phone calls are more personal.

Tate Ortiz (21) – Personally, I think phone calls are better. If I message someone on Twitter or post something on Facebook, nobody knows how I felt when I sent that or posted it. With a phone call, you can hear emotions. Social media is great for saying facts but not for expressing feelings.

Chapter 3

Do You Want to be Right or Left (Disconnected)?

Around seven years ago, I began feeling a disconnect between me and my oldest daughter. I assumed it was largely because my 'little girl' was becoming a woman. The disconnect was due to that, as well as her sudden interests and ambitions in life. It was all because she had changed and it had nothing to do with me, or so I thought.

She was 15 years old at the time and had been accepted to join Florida Dance Theater. She received some scholarships but there was still some of *my* hard-earned money paying for her competitive dance lessons. Not to mention the gas money that it took to get her to and from school. Then there was the time.

As a mortgage broker, my schedule was flexible, so it made more sense for me to drop her off and pick her up. My chauffeur gig would allow my wife to stay focused on the other three children that we homeschooled. The first issue to arise was the start time of the studio. My territory was between Lakeland and Tampa. We lived in Lakeland and I couldn't drop her off until 8 a.m. each morning. It was inconvenient for me to drop her off and head into the office to start my day. That put me *way* behind on my schedule. Not really, but that's what my selfish heart screamed, over and over, every morning I got into the car.

Looking back on that time, I can now see that the disconnect between me and my daughter was largely due to the megaphone and soapbox that I allowed my selfish heart to reside on during that time. Everything was eventually exposed, as it usually is. My wife recognized the forming disconnect and so sweetly called me out by asking me to take notice and find a way to fix it.

Fix it? Did she understand that my daughter was the issue and not me? My daughter didn't even seem to appreciate or understand that I had adjusted my entire schedule and life to accommodate what she wanted to do. I took my stance and defended my position. I was a good dad and I was sacrificing a lot for my daughter to chase her dream. I was sacrificing money, time, and…well, you know…money and time! She didn't even act like she was grateful. (Not really sure thanking me every minute of every day would have satisfied my selfish pride, but I didn't recognize that at the time.)

My wife let me finish my rant before she agreed that I was right. I was a really good dad and I was making lots of sacrifices to ensure our daughter's success. Then she asked me a question that sucker-punched me in the ego, "But, do you want to be right or do you want to be connected?"

Around the same time, I was reading a book by John Eldridge called "Wild at Heart." He said every little girl wanted these questions answered, "Am I beautiful? Am I worth fighting for?" I had to ask myself the hard question. Was I assuring my daughter of this, by acting like she was a burden on my life? Sadly, no!

It was time to kick the soapbox and throw the megaphone. I had to quiet my selfish heart and find a way to connect with my daughter, before things got worse. Just like my associate pastor that I came to befriend, my daughter was also a person and I had to get to know her, instead of thinking about myself and my opinions.

Music has always been something that my family enjoyed. Don't ask any of us to sing or play an instrument but we love to dance and have fun with music. We had dance party Sundays at the house when the kids were younger. During those parties, we would put on some old music, dance around, and laugh. Sometimes *at* each other and sometimes *with* each other.

My daughter and I began listening to music in the car and one day I suggested recording it. That's what all the kids were into, right? Recording funny moments? At first, we just recorded videos to watch them back and laugh at ourselves but then one day we decided to post a video on Facebook and see what would happen. This was the beginning of what would come to be known as 'Morning Drive with Makenna.'

Shooting the videos gave us something to connect with. We enjoyed spending this time laughing and having fun with each other and posting them allowed us to share that joy with others. These light moments of fun in the car opened opportunities for much deeper conversations later down the road. It was the necessary foundation for rebuilding a relationship where my daughter could trust me again with her heart.

FAMILY CHAT

Q – Makenna, did you feel that disconnect talked about in this chapter?

Makenna Ortiz (23) – Dad was so busy working and I never really had the opportunity to spend time with him. My mom would take me places, so naturally she became my preferred person, or parent, because she was with me all the time. I think my relationship with dad really started to change my senior year of high school. When I changed dance studios, it was right by my dad's office, so my mom said he was going to take me to the classes. I got my driver's license late, so I didn't have a choice.

Q – Makenna, what did those morning drives mean to you?

Makenna Ortiz (23) – At first, it was really awkward. Just because you're family doesn't mean you're friends. We were like two strangers in the car every morning. There was a lot of silence and listening to the radio. In my mind, I thought, "I don't want to get to know you, you should get to know me." And, that's just what he did. My dad entered my world. He started asking me questions about my day, my life, dance, etc. and then he started joining in with me, dancing to the radio.

When we first started riding together, I was like, "Okay I'm stuck with you driving me to dance class for a year, great." But, looking back now, I can see how being forced to be together allowed room for conversations.

Q – Has social media helped you build relationships? If so, in what way?

Brycen Ortiz (18) – In certain ways it has. What I love about Instagram is that my buddies and I have this group chat, where we send dumb videos to each other and stay connected with each other. I'm not a big texter but, going into college, I've had to stay connected to my new team and I have been able to do so with Snapchat and Instagram.

Tate Ortiz (21) – I'd say that it has. There are people I've only met one or two times in person. Then, I ended up in a group Snapchat with them or see them on TikTok. So, when I see them again in real life, I am able to know kind of what they have been up to rather than not knowing anything to talk about.

Chapter 4

On-Stage vs. Backstage

As with all things, there must be balance. With social media, it is important that we are always checking our motives. What starts out as just one comment or just one post can soon turn into an obligation to comment or post. Will I let someone down if I don't say something? There were so many people interested in the last video, how will I top that? Will they stop following me if I stop posting for a few days?

Makenna and I certainly found ourselves hitting this point. We began posting as a fun way to connect and repair our relationship. We sang along to songs and talked about life, while the camera happened to be recording. We never asked for a following of 700 viewers encouraging us each post with their likes.

But, sadly, this is the social media net so many people fall into, especially younger people. It starts with one post. You decided to be brave for a change and post something just because you wanted to, just because it was a happy memory or a good time. You got more likes than you had anticipated and suddenly you feel obligated to post again. Well, I was just having fun at first but now that I know people are paying attention, I don't want to let them down.

Makenna and I had fallen for it hook, line, and sinker. Ok, I'll be honest, it was all me. There were a few times that I foolishly recorded CD's (yes, once again dating myself) with songs that I thought would 'connect with our audience.' Connect with our audience? How had this father/daughter bonding moment suddenly turned into a business venture?

I will never forget the day Makenna asked, "Can we not record today?"

"Not record? There are people expecting to see us this morning." I replied, not realizing at the time how silly I must have sounded. I pressed, "But I have this really cool list of songs."

She was not having any of it and, in one moment, I realized that I'd lost sight of why we had even began doing this in the first place. I had forgotten that it was meant for us to connect and have fun.

Once again, I went to my wife to let her know what was going on. I had once again missed the mark and needed her counsel. She reminded me why we had initially started lip-syncing in the car. It was about creating memories; it was about connection.

Makenna and I went back to lip-syncing and belting out our favorite songs on our drives. But the 'performances' were no longer about pleasing an audience, they were back to father and daughter having fun together, connecting.

Eventually, the camera started recording again but only if she initiated it. There were times that I asked if I could post the videos. It was no longer about likes and views. It was about connecting and remembering. I had found a way to connect with my daughter, to have fun with my daughter. I wanted to add the memory to my page like grandma would add a printed photo to her album. I wanted to remember the fun time we had and be able to look back on that memory later down the road.

Can you imagine if we all viewed social media that way? Not as a platform to voice our opinions but just the same as 'Grandma's photo album collection.' Memories to look back on and 'remember that time.' Grandma never stuck a photo of a missed electric bill in the album. She never stuck every nasty thing that she wanted to say to 'Uncle Oddball' there. Her photo albums were books that anyone could open up and 'remember that time.' Anyone could remember those that were no longer with them or 'that one time' that someone decided to 'wear that.'

Switching from 'on-stage' to 'backstage access' wasn't an easy adjustment for me. But this wakeup call certainly helped me recognize that there was a vast difference between needing to share and wanting to share. Nobody really needed me to share anything on social media. The new question in my mind was, "What do I *want* to share on social media?"

This helped me recognize how technology could be used as a tool to preserve precious moments and memories.

FAMILY CHAT

Q – Makenna, when do you feel it switched from having fun to performing?

Makenna Ortiz (23) – During that year we drove to dance class, we had a lot of fun recording and posting. We were just having fun not thinking about the likes. That is just what we did to bond Monday through Friday. It started off a little awkward, because I had a closer relationship with my mom. But, eventually, we grew closer and the videos were an extension of that closer bond we had developed.

Then I went to college and wasn't home for long periods of time. When I came back to visit from college, we would record videos. These videos felt a little awkward. The close bond that we had during our drives to and from dance class wasn't there anymore. It was still a fun way to connect but didn't have the same effect it had on our drives.

When I moved back home after college, there was more pressure to record videos. I no longer felt like we were having a relationship off camera. I'm the type of person that if it doesn't feel authentic, I don't want a part of it. At that point, we're only hanging out to film and get likes and I didn't agree with that.

Q – Do you feel the need to 'perform' on social media? Why or why not?

Tate Ortiz (21) – I definitely used to. But, now, I don't. I realized that no one actually cares. I could post a picture of a dog and get hundreds of likes. So often, I scroll through a ton of posts within minutes and that makes me realize that I shouldn't be posting for anyone but myself. What do I want to share?

Brycen Ortiz (18) – I did at first. Just looking at everyone's posts, I felt like I had to put on an act of what my life was. As time has gone on, I've had to realize that it wasn't who I was. Most of my social media page now is lacrosse and my family. That's what is important in my life. The authentic stuff is stuff that people need to see. It's the stuff they appreciate more.

Chapter 5

It's Not the Devil, Mama

Parents, like it or not, technology is here to stay. With that, the way we connect with others has evolved and we are not turning back anytime soon. As the crazy baboon on Disney's *The Lion King* says, "We can either run from it or learn from it." Running from it is about as absurd as Mama telling Bobby Boucher that everything is the devil throughout Adam Sandler's *The WaterBoy*. Benjamin Franklin? The devil! Football? The devil! And, so on and so on. Social media and technology are not the devil. Or better put, they are not the problem.

The problem is that most of us are stuck on the nostalgias of the past. Remember when people made phone calls, wrote letters, passed notes in class? Those were the good ol' days, right? I'll talk about the 'good ol' days' in a later chapter. For now, I want to talk about how we can stop fighting the advances in technology and learn to use them to our advantage in our relationships. The first of those relationships is being with our children.

Social media is here to stay whether we like it or not. Our jobs as parents doesn't change now that social media is present. We still need to set healthy boundaries for our children to help keep them safe. For my parents, healthy boundaries were telling me, "Be home before the street lights come on." Well, you can't really say that to children that spend the majority of time inside. So, what do healthy boundaries with technology look like?

My wife and I believe setting boundaries and limitations should reflect our family values. As with anything in parenting, this is a judgment-free zone, from one parent to another. There are boundaries that I'm about to list that you may not agree with and that's okay. All I'm saying is find the right boundaries to set for you and your household. Because, no boundaries are no good. Kids need boundaries. Heck, even us adults need boundaries!

Here are some boundaries we've found that work for us and why we use them:

- No cell phone service until you're 15 years old.

I know, this sounds like madness. How will I know where my kid is if they don't have a phone? How will they stay connected with their friends? Isn't it cruel of me to deprive them of this privilege? No! Because that is exactly what having a phone is, a privilege. And with that privilege comes responsibility. My wife and I love using social media to connect. But, we believe even more strongly in protecting and keeping our kids, KIDS, for as long as possible. Having a cell phone, even with restrictions, before they are 15 years old is just more responsibility than they need to worry about at that time.

- Passwords and accessibility.

We have passwords to all our kids' accounts and phones. However, they also have access to ours. Yes, you read that right. My kids have the password to get into my phone. Why would we do that? Because, I want my children to understand the importance of integrity and accountability. There shouldn't be anything to hide. Their friends are less likely to send them inappropriate things when they know they have parents that can access their device and apps at any time. There's safety in integrity. I have co-workers that know my children have access to my phone so they think twice about stuff they send me. If I expect something of my children, I've got to be the first to set the example. That's just my opinion.

- The importance of 'checking-in' and 'checking-out.'

Makenna, my oldest daughter, has this amazing habit of setting her phone to airplane mode while she is with friends. I respect that and am proud of her for ensuring that those people are her sole focus while she is with them – no distractions from phone calls, text messages, or other alerts. Unfortunately, the good habit had a bad effect one night when we could not get in touch with her. When she finally got back to the house, we discussed the importance of 'checking-in.' I reminded her of all the times that I would call her mother to let her know that I would be running late from work or my plans had changed. I did this so that she wouldn't worry. 'Checking-in' wasn't about us keeping tabs on her. It was more about us being informed. Knowing where someone is going to be and about how long they will be there, puts a person's mind at ease. Whereas, no 'check-ins' or updates regarding plans, combined with a phone set to airplane mode or vibrate, produces nothing but needless worry, followed by relationship strain.

- Proper technology etiquette.

Okay, this one isn't a boundary but certainly needs to be taught to our children. Rather than saying, 'no, no, no' we need to be willing to set the example and educate them on the importance of the example we have set. Comment threads and text messages are great but there are still some messages that should be delivered via a phone call. There are also things that you should not post, because it will project the wrong image of who you are. I'm working on this book during the 2020 COVID-19 quarantine and something I have come to appreciate is video messaging. Text on screens causes us to lose some emotion in conversations. And, it is important to keep emotional connection alive.

- Learn their apps.

The biggest thing I hear parents say is that, "I just don't understand all that (insert whatever here)." Well, to that I say, "Don't be afraid to learn. Sign into the apps that they are interested in and using. Learn what is good and bad about the apps, so you can talk through these things with your children. Give them some freedom to make choices." One example, Snapchat had a location feature on it that I had to talk through with my kids. It was a great feature, if you were at the mall and posted something, because it would show you other friends who were near the mall as well that you may not have known were there. The downfall to the feature is that ANYBODY with the app could see where you were at. We discussed how this could be a dangerous thing with our kids and why it was safer to leave their location off the Snapchat posts.

- Don't chat with strangers / sliding into the DM

Whether you realize it or not, your kids are probably using technology at school as well. They have email accounts they use to communicate with their teachers and they attend a few assemblies a year about how to stay safe with technology. Learn what they are being told at school. That is a great place to start with boundaries. They are already being told the dangers of chatting with strangers. If you know the programs, games, and apps they are using, you are more likely able to show them how to shut off chat options and adjust other options for their safety.

- Friend their friends

We friend our kids on their social media networks but we also friend their friends. It allows us to see who they are hanging out with, what kind of kids they are, and what kind of influence they might have in our kids' lives. I remember a while back, my son's friend posted a picture of my son on our roof. I called my son and asked him why in the world he was on the roof. Let's go back to accountability and integrity. I'm not saying to become best friends and chat it up with your kid's friends. All I am saying is be their friend, so you have insight to who they are and what they stand for. And, maybe which ones are climbing on the roof to impress their friends.

I can't say it enough, in my opinion, we would do ourselves a lot of good by spending a lot less time criticizing these platforms and apps our kids live on. We need to spend more time engaging with them and learning to communicate with our kids and their friends on their "turf." I know, I know, back in my day we would play outside until the street lights came on. We tend to glorify the past and vilify the future. The past was our glory days but for some reason we forget to allow our kids to experience their own glory days. I would argue that, with all the different ways to connect, our kids' generation is actually more connected than we were.

Physical activity is important. All of our kids have played sports and have been involved in all sorts of extracurricular things. However, kids are still connecting. I know, when we were kids, we did it by being gone all day with our buddies. Today, they do it by playing NBA 2K or Fortnite with their friends online. Don't tell me this isn't real interaction.

One of my favorite things to hear is our 12-year-old, Morgan, in the middle of a Fortnite online battle with Tate, our 21 year old, who is away at college in Tennessee. Morgan will be on fire, taking down people on the opposing team. And, one of Tate's college buddies will inevitably say, "Who is that playing with you?"

To which our 21-year-old will proudly say, "My 12-year-old brother."

Technology provides them an opportunity to step into each other's lives, while being physically separated. I can tell you, my boys' relationship with each other have improved because of it. There is no replacement for physical contact. Parents, our kids very much need to appreciate face-to-face interactions with their friends. But technology can bridge the gap, when physical contact is not an option. COVID 19 has taught us this, with the use of Zoom to connect with family when we all our cities were shutdown.

My recommendation is to allow your kids to plug in. Teach them the importance of face-to-face meetings. Guide them in all forms of communication, because it will greatly benefit them. Set boundaries and, above all, get to know what they are interested in. Do your homework parents! Learn those apps and don't be afraid to dive into "their" world.

FAMILY CHAT

Q – How did you feel about the boundaries your parents set growing up?

Makenna Ortiz (23) – First of all, I'm the oldest, so I feel like I'm typically the guinea pig for their parenting. But, I appreciated the boundaries my parents set, because they were my cop out. It was easy to say that I couldn't date until I was 16 years old, because it was my parents' rule. It was easy to say that I shouldn't post something, because my parents had access to my accounts. Obviously, that doesn't work when you get older. But it helps navigate a lot of the decision-making during those awkward teen years, when you're still trying to figure things out.

And, really, I didn't need a phone before I was 16 years old. I was homeschooled and I didn't have a license. So, I think that makes me a little different. I think if I have a kid and they're going to school, then I may have some different standards, because I would want to be able to get in touch with my kid. But, I wasn't too upset with that boundary, because it made sense, since I was typically with one of my parents.

I think that since my parents were so technology savvy, it detoured me from being sneaky or posting stuff I shouldn't. I never thought to do those things, because I didn't have anything I wanted to hide.

Morgan Ortiz (12) – I think they're completely fine. I understand everything. Time limit wise, I'm fine with that. They just want me to exercise more and get out and I'm completely fine with that.

Brycen Ortiz (18) – At a younger age I didn't get it and I didn't like it. I'm the third youngest, so I wanted all these things. There were a couple of things that they bent a little and I think it happens that way as parents learn new things. I traveled a lot with sports, so they allowed me to get a phone when I was 14 years old. Now that I'm older, I understand the boundaries they set a little more. But, there are still some that I don't understand. Having a younger brother has allowed me to see why those boundaries are good though.

Tate Ortiz (21) – It's a little weird. When I was growing up, the first game console I had was PlayStation 2. There were boundaries, even with that, but I don't think I really realized how restricted we were, because Facebook was generally new when I was growing up.

Q – Jennifer, as a mother, what do boundaries look like with your children in regards to technology and social platforms?

Jennifer Ortiz – We try to set a time limit, especially with the older ones. It's hard with four kids, because you get busier. We always had access to our kids' phones and they knew that we could ask to check them at any time. I think, because we set those boundaries before they had phones or tablets or anything, it wasn't a fight when it happened. Because we had access, there were certain pages or channels that they were not allowed to follow or download.

Q – How do you determine what apps are good and what apps are bad for your kids?

Jennifer Ortiz – We observe how the apps are affecting them and then decide if it is something that needs to be taken away.

Q – Do you use the same standard for all the kids or are there different standards for different kids?

Jennifer Ortiz – We have three boys and a girl. So, I think it would be a little difficult to set different standards. For us, if it was a no for one of them, it was a no for all of them, just to keep it uniformed across the board. Now, when our boys got older, they started buying their own games and things like that. We had to keep that in mind. The teens could play some games when their younger brother went to bed.

Q – What is your advice for parents who want to friend their children's friends on social media? What boundaries do you have for them?

Jennifer Ortiz – My kids' friends would like me on Facebook and Instagram and that's fine, because I have a lot of family-oriented stuff. But, I didn't like them back. That was a boundary for me. Like, right now, I would not follow any of Morgan's friends, because he is 12 years old and I am still his parent. But with our other kids that are older, I am more of a mentor, so I can mentor their friends as well.

I would say I probably didn't follow anyone back until they got to high school. At that point, their friends were spending a lot of time with our family, I would follow them back, so I could see what my kids were doing with their friends. My green light was certainly not liking/following until they liked/followed me first.

That's a given in social media, right? You know that if you follow somebody, chances are, they will want to follow you back. I figured if they were following me, then they were fine with me following them back.

I just want to encourage kids. When it came to my kids' friends, I knew a lot of their stories and was aware when they were having hard times. I just wanted to be a positive light and tell them they were beautiful and doing a great job along the way.

Q – What are the benefits of having boundaries vs. downfalls of not having boundaries?

Jennifer Ortiz – I think when you don't have boundaries, it's just an invitation for chaos. Parents, when there aren't boundaries, they lose control. Danny and I talked about how we wanted to parent, before we had kids. Such as the big things, like we don't want them to date until they are 16 years old. We knew these things, so we could start talking to them at a very young age. It sets expectations but it also brings peace. They're going to fight you on things. But, when they know what the boundaries are, and they know that you stick by them, it brings peace.

Q – Do you ever get friend requests from a friend's parent? Is it weird?

Brycen Ortiz (18) – Yeah, I have a couple of my friends' parents on Snapchat. I never thought it was weird, because I never posted anything incriminating. There was some stuff that I might have posted and my dad would tell me not to post it or delete the post. He was protecting me, because I had posted it, but didn't understand how other people might take it.

Tate Ortiz (21) – Yeah, I felt like I couldn't decline them, because I would see them occasionally in real life. You get a request, 'hey I'm on Facebook now' and you feel like you can't say no, because you may run into them. I think that's why a bunch of kids in my generation left Facebook, because our parents and grandparents got a Facebook page.

Chapter 6

Navigating the Negative

I'd like to move on to other relationships and how we can use social media to build those relationships. But, I would have to count it as a major loss if I did not stop here for a moment to recognize the negative effect that social media can have, especially on our children. Since we talked about setting boundaries in the last chapter, I'd like to take this chapter to talk about the dark alleys of technology and social media. The places that we would never EVER dream to allow our children to roam in the real world but all too often unknowingly allow them to roam on the internet. Here are some things that we need to be cautious of when it comes to the internet and social media platforms.

1) Strangers are Still Strangers

Something that has not changed over the years is this advice that parents and loving adult mentors have provided to children in saying, "Never ever talk to strangers."

While that is still very much used in today's world, I think that it has become lost a little in the tech world. It is all too easy to start up a chat on a social media platform or online game. Some kids might red flag it right off the bat, but others begin to evaluate it. The person on the other side of the screen isn't quite real to them. For some of them, chatting online gets categorized in their mind with asking Siri questions. They haven't seen this other person, so there isn't really a threat.

Parents, grandparents, adults, and older siblings across the board – we must be vigilant to guard young people against this kind of prowling. It doesn't matter if 'Gamer123' was chatting with you about a level. You don't know who the person on the other end really is, so it is better to keep your guard up. Please, please, stress to your children the importance of never ever giving out their personal information.

And I will take that just a step further to say we as adults must also be aware of what information we are sharing and with who. If a random person called you, the chances of you chatting it up with them is slim. But, if someone in a cooking group begins having DM conversations with you, it may not seem as strange. Be diligent to guard your kids, as well as yourselves.

2.) This is Me – Our Personal Brand

Another thing to be cautious about is the image we are projecting. Your reputation, or as they call it today, your personal brand is, like it or not, directly tied to how you portray yourself online today. I've had many conversations with my children about how they are branding themselves through social media. I often let them know everything you post online is permanent. Their push back is often, "Well, dad, it goes away after 24 hours on platforms like Snap and Insta Stories." I quickly point them to the stories of many in positions of leadership whose careers have been wrecked by a post they put online, then changed their mind about and took down. However, some follower took a screen shot of it and reposted it. We are all doing this, whether we intend to or not. What we post, share, and like is a reflection of what we believe and who we are. That is awful, because sometimes we post stuff and have no idea that it is taken in a much different way on the other side. I've had my kids remove stuff from their social media platforms, because while they thought it was funny it could be taken in a much different light.

Anything that we post on social media has the opportunity of becoming our personal resume. Businesses often look at people's social media accounts to evaluate what kind of person they are. If you're constantly posting how terrible your current job is on social media, what kind of image would that present to a recruiter? We are branded by what we post, whether we like it or not. For this reason, it is very important that we educate and help our children navigate what they are and are not posting. It is also vitally important that we, ourselves, evaluate what we are posting. So, am I telling you to be a fake person online? Nope, that's not what I am saying. As I often put it to my kids, "If you want to post that particular thing you must be prepared to deal with the fallout – good or bad. And, if you are comfortable with that, go right ahead." It's just that we have never lived in a world where a thought can go from your head into social media platforms in the span of 30 seconds. It is like saying something in the heat of the moment, with a friend or family member, that you later regret. It's easier to ask for and get forgiveness when the conversation is private. It's not so easy, when you have put your thoughts and feelings out to the world, to back track and change your story. Just think before you post. Not every thought needs to be out there for the world to see.

3.) The Cyber Bully (I would like to write a little more on this will have to you in a day or so)

Bullies aren't a new thing. There have always been bullies. But with the evolution of technology, bullying has also evolved. Nowadays it's no longer about wedgies and swirlies, instead it is a mental battlefield. A young girl posts a new outfit that she likes. Maybe she receives some likes, maybe she receives a thousand likes. But those likes are overshadowed by negative comments from people criticizing everything about it. Maybe the positive comments greatly outnumber the negative, but negative is still hurtful.

Again, I go back to the keyboard warrior. It is so easy to give an opinion, hit enter, and walk away without another thought. Some cyber bullies do just that. They simply think they have the best opinion and put it out there. However, there are also cyber bullies that intentionally seek out people and harass them via social media. Kids aren't the only victims. There are adults who get bullied as well. We've got to ensure that we are not allowing these people to have that kind of voice in our lives. If someone has nothing but negative things to say to us, then we can start by having an in-person conversation with them. If that doesn't work, we may need to consider unfriending or even blocking the person.

As adults, it may require us being "the bad guy" in the eyes of our child for a moment. Often times, kids are not strong enough to walk away from a bully, so it may come down to you saying an individual needs to be unfriended or blocked.

4.) The Image on the Mirror

This is probably one of the most important negatives that we need to be aware of and guard ourselves against. The Evil Queen from *Snow White and the Seven Dwarfs* constantly asked the mirror who was the most beautiful. If we are not careful, we can use social media in the same way. Who is taking the best vacations? Who is having the most fun in life? Who has mastered parenting? Who should I measure myself against? Who am I doing better than? Who am I not measuring up to?

It is a super vicious web to get caught in and yet so many of us find ourselves trapped without realizing it. Do not use social media sites to compare and measure your life against. That is not what they are meant for.

5.) Living Without Experiencing

The last negative thing that I'm going to touch on is getting wrapped up in this virtual world. It is so easy to scroll for hours without realizing it. Sometimes, just like what happened with me and Makenna, we can get wrapped up in posting something and forget to experience this life we are living. "Let me get this amazing picture and post it really quick." Great, we got 200 pictures of the Grand Canyon that we shared on social media but did we sit down once to enjoy the view without posting anything? We spent an entire day with our spouse or kids but never took the time to converse with them. We got some 'great' pictures but we forgot to see how their life was going. We forgot to experience the people they are.

If everything is about what we will post next, we have lost sight of living. Sharing experiences and memories on social media is great. But, just like 'Grandma's photo album,' let's make sure that picture speaks a thousand words to the people that were there.

FAMILY CHAT

Q – What advice would you give parents regarding technology?

Makenna Ortiz (23) – Parents, it's not as scary as you think it is. The more that you make it out to be a bad thing, the more it will strain your relationship with your child. People are so creative with making videos and my generation loves and appreciates that. You could be inhibiting your child's gifts by making it a bad thing. There's lots of ways to develop a relationship with your children. I didn't need to hide what I was doing from my parents, because I trusted them. Try and get to know your kids' hearts. And, remember that we're gonna figure things out in stages.

Morgan Ortiz (12) – I actually don't even know. My friends' parents are the same as mine. They have a lot of the same rules.

Brycen Ortiz (18) – Be aware of what your kids are posting and what they are looking at. Social media can be positive and negative, but that negativity can really get some kids down. I had a friend that was really torn down by negative comments on social media. It was really hurting her self-esteem until she realized that she didn't need to listen to all that negativity. Also, help them understand what they should and shouldn't post. It can affect if you get a job and things like that. Follow their pages and see what they are posting and guide them through their posting since they are young and don't understand.

Tate Ortiz (21) – I think parents should try to understand technology. It's hard to comprehend things that didn't exist for you. The internet didn't even exist when my dad was my age. Do your best to understand it. Technology is always changing.

Q – How do you deal with negative comments on social media?

Makenna Ortiz (23) – I don't really read the comments. I just post what is authentic for me.

Brycen Ortiz (18) – I've just learned to block them out and move on with my life. It's something I had to learn at a young age, that it is not something that has to affect my life. If I post that I am going to a certain college to play lacrosse some people might say I'm not going to do well. They might say, I'm too short or something. But, I've had to learn that I can't let other people's comments affect my life.

Tate Ortiz (21) – Personally I just tend to ignore them. About three years ago, someone told me if you ever post something, just ignore what people comment – negative or positive. I just swipe clear and never even bother.

Chapter 7

Chillin' on the Back Porch

Technology and social platforms allow us to form closer relationships with our children. When used properly, they give us insight that our parents never had with us. Your child might post that they are having a rough day and you'll be able to use that information to start a conversation with them. Whereas, in the past you might have been shrugged off with an, "I'm fine."

The potential for closer relationships doesn't end with our children. We can use technology as a tool to form closer relationships with everyone in our lives. Deep down, everybody hopes someone cares about who they are and what is going on inside their life. They want to know they are being seen and understood. Sometimes, like the keyboard warrior I described earlier, it is easier to put the information out there, hit enter, and walk away. A lot of kids use social media platforms as outlets to see who's paying attention, who cares enough to look. But, it doesn't end with kids. Adults do the same thing, whether we realize it or not.

All the information we are given by others' social media accounts allows us to drive all the relationships in our lives into a much deeper level. Don't get played by the media. Don't get caught up in likes and followers. Instead, use the platform to tap into the world of others.

By definition that's what it is supposed to be used for:

Social media noun, plural in form but singular or plural in construction

: Forms of electronic communication (such as websites for social networking and microblogging) **through which users create online communities** to share information, ideas, personal messages, and other content (such as videos)[2] **[emphasis added]**

Did you have any idea that person who sits two rows behind you at church loved to cook, before you saw all the mouth-drooling pictures of their meals on Instagram? Probably not.

Did you realize that guy you work with, the one that always wears the fancy suits, goes hiking and camping almost every weekend, before you friended him on Facebook? Probably not.

Why is that? Because we like our personal space. I know it is totally weird. A lot of us have this strange sense of social awkwardness when it comes to letting down our guard and being vulnerable in

---

[2] https://www.merriamwebster.com/dictionary/social%20media

person. But, social networks provide this sort of security blanket that allow us to drop our guards.

Why do we post the things we post? I think it stems from a tribal mindset. As the saying goes, "Birds of a feather flock together." At any given moment, you want to know who your people are. Who enjoys the same things that you do? Where are the committed Ford owners? Who are the diehard Ohio State fans? There are times that we post, because we thoroughly enjoyed something, and we want to share that joy with others. Maybe they will get it, maybe they won't. We post, because we want to connect. At the core of us, we long for relationships and connection. But, more than anything, we want to be accepted for who we are and what we enjoy.

One of the things I enjoy to partake in is smoking a cigar on my front porch. Sometimes I'll do this to unwind after a tough week, other times I'll celebrate a big life event. Either way, it is something I enjoy. You know what makes it even better? When my wife, Jennifer, joins me on the porch. Why do I enjoy it so much? First of all, because I have a smoking hot wife that I enjoy being around, duh. But, aside from that, I enjoy it, because when she steps onto the back porch to join me, she doesn't come with an agenda or 'honey-do' list. She steps onto the back porch to sit and talk with me. She takes a moment to 'step into my world' and accept me how I am.

It is the same thing that I found happening with my daughter, Makenna, on those car rides a few years back. I had to step into her space if I wanted to get to know her and build a relationship with her.

I have recently found myself taking the same approach to others. Like I said, we all want to have connection and be accepted for who we are and what we like. Have you ever run into that person that will talk your ear off about their passion? It doesn't matter what it is, but they will talk and talk. They aren't trying to be annoying, they're just so passionate about something that they want to share it with you.

The thing I often ask myself is how can I connect with others? How can I use their interests to drive more personal relationships? How can I step into others' interests? Step in their space?

I have found one way to do that is to go beyond the text on the screen. Facebook alerts you that it is your friend's birthday, right? Instead of adding to the comment thread why not go one step beyond? Why not send them a text, call them, or even drop off a gift card for them to get coffee?

We need to look at social as a way we can connect with others.

FAMILY CHAT

Q – Can you speak a little about the importance of stepping into someone's space and accepting them as they are in that moment?

Jennifer Ortiz – For any relationship, but especially kids and spouses, you want to maintain connection with them at all costs. Once you lose connection, you lose communication and it spirals from there. For me, it was like why wouldn't I. I may not like cigars, but I love this person. I knew he wanted me out there, because he would often ask me to join him. To me, joining him on the porch was such an easy thing and so simple. It's fun, cause now we can talk about it together. By doing that, I filled his cup and now he is more likely to fill mine. Every decision that Danny and I have done is like 'what is our relationship going to look like when our kids are gone.'

Q – What is your favorite form of communication and why?

Jennifer Ortiz – I definitely enjoy talking face to face. Danny is so good about picking up the phone and staying in touch with old friends. I'd much rather meet up with someone for coffee or something. I also love honest communication. Sometimes, people try not to say things that are too honest, because they're afraid it will hurt your feelings. But, I love honest communication.

Q – Does your form of communication vary depending on who you are communicating with?

Jennifer Ortiz – Absolutely. Each personality is different. I can get excited and loud with Makenna. But, if I get excited with Tate, he asks why I'm yelling at him, so I have to adjust to each of their personalities.

Q – What are a few steps that parents might be able to take to connect with their kids?

Jennifer Ortiz – For me, all I ever wanted to be was a mom. But, I wanted Danny to have a special relationship with them as well. When Makenna got into high school and the other kids needed more attention with home-schooling, I asked Dan if he could take her and have that attention.

The most important thing in my opinion is to look at them as individuals. You can't group them all into one thing. Makenna loved to have fun and dance. Danny loves music, so that is why he started playing old school music in the car. And, they just started having a good time in the car. Then it evolved into songs she liked as well. And, they weren't silent in the car anymore. Once you start building that connection with them, the walls start coming down. With Tate, he is a completely different kid. He started talking politics at 12 years old and I would tell him that his dad would be much better to talk to about that topic. Every parent has something in common with their kid. Even if they feel silly doing it. I don't believe that there is nothing they can find to connect on.

I was so thankful that Tate had Danny, because I could not have those kinds of conversations with him and give him that fulfillment. I could talk about ANYTHING else with him, but politics was what Dan and Tate could have better conversations about.

Chapter 8

You've Got Mail

Gary Vaynerchuck, entrepreneur, author, speaker, and Internet personality, has famously said social media should lead to 'real human interaction.'

How is that possible? If it is possible, why are there so many people complaining about social media destroying human interaction? That goes back to what I said about attacking the messengers and setting boundaries. There are moments that we need to learn to set down or shut down our technology. How do we use the tools we've been given to create real human interaction?

One of the worst things about social media can also be one of the best. Let me explain. The bad part about social media is that it removes the filters we normally use for human interaction. Similar to texting, we are all braver behind a keyboard. We say things when we are hiding behind a keyboard that we would never say to someone who is standing right in front of us.

In a very similar way, we reveal parts of ourselves on social media that we would normally not share if others were standing right in front of us. How many of us have posted something incredibly silly or awkward that we would not do in front of others?

If you are looking to connect and I mean really connect with others, Facebook is a great place for research. It's all right there in front of you, if you just pay attention. Every post, every picture, every comment, every meme tells you something about the people in your life. All these things give you hundreds of topics to start up conversations and help you get to know people deeper. Then, there are the personal things that give you an opportunity to go beyond basic conversation starters. Someone posts that their child is in the hospital, and it gives you an opportunity to call them and pray with them. If you live close enough, it's an opportunity to take them a meal, so there's one less thing for them to think about. Or, maybe someone posts about going through a break-up or divorce. There's an opportunity to be there for that person – in person or through phone conversations. Maybe they don't want advice or your thoughts on the matter, but knowing that they have someone they can call and talk to can be very comforting. Knowing that someone cares is comforting.

Think about the good you can do when you see someone post about having a bad morning and you stop by with a gift card to their favorite coffee shop, while letting them know you hope the rest of their day gets better. Or, you see that your child posted about having a challenge and you use it to start up a conversation about what is going on in their life. Or better yet, DM them within the app they are using to show that you see them and care about them.

I am a big fan of 'taking in' the information I see posted on social media and using it for 'real human interaction.' On Facebook, I love when someone wishes me a 'Happy Birthday.' But, when someone takes an extra two minutes out of their day to call and wish me a 'Happy Birthday,' something happens to me inside with the way I feel about that person. That's especially so in this world where it's all about speed. And, where typically it's about hitting the like button and moving on with the busy day.

If you have seen they had a bad day, go old school and send a card. Yes, I said it! For all the talk about connecting electronically, there is still some nostalgia about receiving something in the mail. Think about how that person feels when they open the mail a few days after they made a post on having a tough day and they get a card from you in the mail with a $5 gift card saying. "I saw you had a bad day. I hope this makes today better for you."

Or, in business, you see on social media that one of your clients' kids just got accepted to a school they are really excited about. Of course, they post about it on Facebook or Instagram and a few days later they open the mail only to find a ballcap from that school, with a note of congratulations.

Or, if you see someone lost someone dear to them, send a text message or pick up the phone and let them know you are grieving with them. You see, the goal isn't just to post or comment. The goal is personal connection. Gary Vaynerchuck wrote about this in his book, *"The Thank you Economy."*

When someone slows down to show another human being that they care, it does something.

FAMILY CHAT

Q – How do you use the information on social media to build better relationships?

Tate Ortiz (21) – I go to school out of state, so the only way I know what my friends are up to is to see what they are doing on social media. Also, I don't have time to memorize everyone's birthday, so having social media remind me is convenient. It helps people feel special showing that you care. I mean, it also eliminates excuses, though, because you can't say you forgot someone's birthday when they can see you went onto social media a bunch of times that day.

Brycen Ortiz (18) – I'm more of a phone-call guy. If I see a friend post something about having a bad day, I will text them and say, "Hey, call me." If they aren't able to call me, then I will send a bunch of funny videos to help cheer them up.

Chapter 9

To Post or Not to Post?

I mentioned earlier that there were times I posted, because I thought I had the best opinion available. Then, when Makenna and I were making videos, I got into a period where I posted to appease the fans. It was an obligation, or duty, to post something. Today, my view on what to post, and when, is very different.

Today I post for many different reasons. One of the first reasons is to leave a legacy.

I think the most unselfish thing you can do as a father is post content and document as much of your life as possible. People warn others to be careful what they post to the internet, because 'that stuff never goes away.' If that's the case, let's use it for good. What we post will outlive us and will be out there for our children, grandchildren, great grandchildren and so on. I would love to have more videos of my mom and dad now that they have passed away. Pictures may be worth a thousand words, but videos are priceless. My dad was a chef by trade, and what I wouldn't give to just have him on video showing us how he me made some of the best meals we enjoyed as a family. My mom had a radio show on the airwaves in Orlando for years and to have footage of her on the air with her callers would be priceless. There's nothing like hearing someone's laugh one more time.

One of the reasons I post so much is because my kids will have a video legacy of what their dad was like. For that reason, I am personally working on being more vulnerable on camera with important topics, so that they can be reminded about what my values were after I am gone.

Another reason I post is to allow topic starters with other people and tear down stereotypes.

In the last couple years, the Lord has really been working on me to release myself from people's judgment. There were times when I would be 'guilted' by other husbands, because my wife posted something nice I did for her. Or, because I posted about how amazing my wife was. These guys would say, "Dude, you're making us look bad." Receiving those comments would sometimes make me feel like I wasn't living up to a manly image, and that maybe I was being too soft. But, deep down I knew I loved my wife and didn't care how soft I looked when loving on her through the words I posted.

When I receive comments like this today, I just tell them the truth, "If that's the case then maybe you need to 'Up your game' and celebrate your wife more. Because, I'm not trying to make anybody look bad, I'm just loving my wife with all I've got and celebrating our life together."

I think that is what sparked our front porch talks we have recently started recording and posting on Facebook. All too often, we hear couples acting like they are trapped in their marriage. You know, the stereotypical thought of the bachelor party being the last hoorah, the last day of your life. That's so not true. Marriage and family can be fun. Yes, there are moments that aren't fun. But, dammit, you're going to be together for the rest of your lives, so make it a nice ride instead of making each other miserable.

My wife and I have had moments where we 'opened up' and talked about personal subjects. Is it sometimes uncomfortable? Yes, because you never know how people are going to receive what you say. But in all honesty, it has opened some really great opportunities for us to speak into others' lives. There have been many people who private message us, because of a topic that we speak about. They have asked us to pray for their kids or marriage. Some have sought our counsel. Some we've redirected to professional counselors to ensure they had help we were unable to provide.

We want to encourage dads to be involved. Look at me, I needed that advice to connect with Makenna before it was too late. We also want to encourage couples to have fun and enjoy life together. At the end of the day, our measure of whether or not we should post something is whether or not it will bring value to someone else's life. Will it be something wonderful for our kids to look back on and remember? Will it spark a long overdue conversation between two people? Will it give encouragement to someone at the end of their rope?

FAMILY CHAT

Q – Does anyone have anything to comment on this section?

crickets

Chapter 10

Market Like a Gen Z

I never thought that what I post on social media could also benefit my business. I take my wife to as many business events as I can. I want people to know that I am a family man. I want them to know that my wife is important to me. That message spills over onto my social media as well with our front-porch talks. People know that the Dan they see in person is the same Dan they'll see on social media. My image doesn't change. I believe that is one of the biggest reasons that female realtors feel comfortable contacting me. I mean, you never know if someone is a creeper. Seeing my vulnerable talks with my wife shows them that my family and my marriage is important to me. They can ask me business questions without wondering if there are hidden agendas lurking in the background. This only happens, because I'm authentic with who I am on and off camera.

Using social media for business purposes has exploded over the past few years. I think the reason that it works so well is because it humanizes the person posting. A billboard or TV commercial doesn't have the same affect. With social media, you're not just a realtor or salesman or doctor, you're a person with a personality.

There are many ways that business professionals are getting creative for their clients and with their clients. I have two friends that offered to provide interviews for this chapter. One is a dentist that began creating TikTok videos with his patients for fun. Something that was meant for fun exploded into a great way to connect with his patients and draw in new patients. But, don't take my word for it, let's see what he has to say.

Q – When and why did you start making TikTok videos with your patients?

Dr. Brian Beard – Well, for the last three years, on Halloween we always had fun. We would have themes. The first year we did a Soul Train 70's theme. We posted a video on Facebook and people went crazy. People were like, "I want to be there next year." Next year, Run DMC was the theme and this past year Post Malone. Someone told me we should really start using TikTok. I had no idea what it was, so I started looking at it. And, it seemed like the perfect thing to do.

Q – What benefit have you seen in creating these videos versus using conventional advertising?

Dr. Brian Beard – It's just amazing. Honestly, every day, all day long, I'm hearing about TikTok, no matter where I go. I was at Petco and some ladies were walking into Ulta, beside it. They asked if I could do a TikTok with them. I was in a hurry, so I couldn't that day. but she told me that she wanted to bring her husband to me to get his veneers done, because she wanted to do a TikTok video with me. That's a pretty big procedure and she wants to bring the business to me all because of TikTok. And, stuff like this happens every day.

I think it makes our office a fun place to be. We just won "Best of the Best" dentist office this year, 2020. I think it has a lot to do with the TikTok videos and the fun environment that we've created.

Most of them are dancing but I also put some before/after pictures and follow with a dance video. People all the time are commenting, "I wish my dentist was as cool as you." "Where are you located?" I actually had a 12-year-old girl that I pulled out a baby tooth on a couple months back who sent me a message and asked me when she could come back in to pull another tooth and do another TikTok. It took me a couple days to reply, so by the time I did there was a follow-up with a bunch of questions marks. How many 12-year-olds do you know chasing down their dentist to get a tooth pulled?

Q – What advice would you give other business professionals that are thinking of using social media to promote their business?

Dr. Brian Beard – Remember that you're a professional. I think that is the biggest thing I try to do with TikTok, for the most part. I'm always trying to find the clean version of songs.

Remember that you're a professional. You don't want to do anything to hurt your image. Also, use other platforms. I post the videos across Facebook and Instagram. The majority of my patients don't have TikTok but their kids do and somehow, I'm TikTok famous. When you do all three of these media sites, you're reaching all generations.

Q – If someone would have told you early in your practice that you'd be making videos with your patients, would you have believed them?

Dr. Brian Beard – Kind of, yeah. I would have never thought it would be like this. But, I always liked to dance and always liked music. I've always been good with marketing and finding out what my patients like. If I was told about it in dental school, I would have been excited to go for it.

> FB- http://www.facebook.com/brian.k.beard
> IG- http://www.instagram.com/briankbeard
> TikTok @drbrianccd

Who would have thought that posting short dance videos on TikTok would have patients chasing down their dentist to set up appointments? That is the power of social media that can be tapped in to use for good. Power given to use to build better working relationships.

Another friend of mine decided to begin posting daily Facebook videos. As a lawyer, he realized that people have lots of questions about laws and their rights.

Q – When did you decide to start posting Facebook videos?

Edward Reyes – I started doing it more when I was in real estate. I was posting Facebook videos, because I knew I was going to law school. I needed people to get to know me better, so it wasn't a big shock to people. It was to build a personal brand.

Q – When you posted your first video, did you think it would turn into what it is today?

Edward Reyes – No not even close. I always did short videos here and there. I started doing morning shows, so people could get to know me, like me, and trust me. At first, I was dry mouth and nervous and awkward, but now it's routine. We get a lot of recommendations and new clients because of the posts.

Q – What benefit do you see these videos having for you as a lawyer and for your clients that are viewing them?

Edward Reyes – I think that the clients feel more connected, like I'm their friend. It's kind of the same thing as reality stars. It's made my business a lot more lucrative.

Q – Has posting videos changed or affected your practice? If so, in what ways?

Edward Reyes – It's gotten me a lot of referrals each day. As we close with clients, those clients refer new clients. We take a lot of picture throughout the process, so people see their friends and family getting paid and the service rendered. So, then, if they need a lawyer they're more likely to come to me.

Q – What advice would you give other business professionals who are thinking about using social media for marketing?

Edward Reyes – Be constant. Continue, especially, when you think it is not working. There are other platforms that I want to get on but I'm not doing as well, because I'm not constant on them. The ones that I am constant on are the ones that are working the best. I post multiple times a day on multiple platforms.

The Reyes Firm
813-421-3411
www.TheReyesFirm.com
DM: http://M.me/thereyesfirm
IG: www.instagram.com/EdwardReyes_
FB: www.facebook.com/thereyesfrim
YouTube: http://bit.ly/TheReyesFirmVideos

FAMILY CHAT

Q – How would you feel if your dentist posted TikTok videos with his patients?

Jennifer Ortiz – I think I would get a kick out of it. I'd look at it and think, "I wish I was that brave to not care, but just have fun with your patients or friends." I think it sets yourself apart because people don't do that.

Makenna Ortiz (23) – I would see it as a smart marketing tool. Because, the younger generation is ultimately what is driving the world today, which means that you have the choice to either jump in or miss out.

Morgan Ortiz (12) – Honestly, I don't know really. If I was asked to do it I probably wouldn't, but I think it would be fine if other people wanted to.

Tate Ortiz (21) – I think it really does lighten the mood. That being said, I think the only reason he gets away with it is because he's a good dentist. If he was a bad dentist and he was making TikToks, people would just think he was goofing off.

Brycen Ortiz (18) – I think it is a great way to help get your company noticed and your skills. It also shows how relatable you are to the younger generation, which will bring more business.

Q – What are the best ways you've seen businesses use social media to promote their services or products?

Jennifer Ortiz – I love examples. Don't just promote a product and not give an example of how it works. I wanna know if it works before I buy it. But, if I'm watching a video and someone keeps saying, "You can find this in my book," Constantly plugging their product it annoys me. Teach me how to use it, don't just tell me to buy it.

Tate Ortiz (21) – I think Instagram ads and podcast advertisements are definitely the best way to promote products. Personally, I've never bought more products in my life than I have from Podcasts I listen to and ads I see on Instagram. They might be listening to me through my microphone, but they always give me what I need when I need it.

Makenna Ortiz (23) – By using ads on Instagram, but also strategically engaging with the followers. Because, it's one thing to post it and leave it, but it's another to interact and feel like you're part of the cause/conversation/brand.

Brycen Ortiz (18) – A lot of companies use Instagram, Snapchat, etc. A big thing I've noticed, at times, is that they will use, or grab, popular influencers to help promote their product or brand.

Q – Are there any ways that businesses overdo it on social networks? Are there ways they annoy you as a consumer by utilizing social media?

Jennifer Ortiz – I think the people that do a good job selling something are those that are natural, they are being themselves. People see through people, read people and spot fake.

Tate Ortiz (21) – Yeah, I think a lot of ads on social media aren't designed for the platform that they're on. You'll see a business putting the same ad up on Facebook that they did on Twitter. And, it makes no sense, because a different kind of person is on Twitter than is on Facebook.

Brycen Ortiz (18) – Yes, some companies might overdo it on their own with platforms like Instagram or Snapchat and spam their product. At that point, for a consumer-like myself, I don't even want to give the product a chance. There is a big difference between overdoing it and doing it just right.

Makenna Ortiz (23) – Honestly, at the end of the day I respect the hustle. Because, using free platforms on social media to promote a business is extremely hard work. So, personally, I don't mind when I get flooded with someone's business page content on multiple platforms, because I know it probably took a lot of strategy and time.

Chapter 11

Above All Else, Just Get Connected

The moral of the story is that we have so many ways to connect with other people in this day and age. However, we do have to try even harder to connect. People senselessly throw stuff onto social media to get it out of their mind. Others post stuff to see who might be paying attention. At the end of the day, it is all about people. Appreciate people, respect people, connect with people.

Is there bad stuff involved with social media and technology? Of course, there is. I could probably pull up a list of statistics that state the amount of suicides linked to bullying through social media. I could probably pull up other statistics about family disconnect since technology came about. But, you know what the truth is, there were zero automobile accidents before automobiles were invented. In the years that followed the invention of the automobile, guess what, there were automobile accidents.

Everything has a positive and negative side to it. Even my wife and kids repeated that over and over throughout the **FAMILY CHAT** sections of this book. Social media can be a dark, lonely place for people that are going there to seek connection, to seek relationships. These social platforms cannot be our 'one-and-done places' to create and build relationships. We must have real-life human interaction. We must not forget that we are human beings with emotions. We feel happy, sad, joyful, grateful, lonely, and so much more. We need other people around us to experience these feelings with us.

Like I mentioned before, I started writing this book and suddenly the world was on lockdown because of COVID-19. This event changed how we connect and why we connect. There have been so many commercials that have aired during this time that have stated, "You're not alone, we're in this together." Why? Because we need to know there is a person on the other side of the screen. We need to never ever forget that as human beings, we were created for connection.

Before we part ways, I'd like to give you some practical points to evaluate how you currently use social media and how you can use it going forward.

1) Pretend You Don't Know You

Look at your social media accounts from an outsider's view. If you weren't "you," what would you think about the things you post? Honestly.

2) Look Beyond the Posts

Examine your friends and family's social media accounts. What kind of things really matter to them? What do they talk about more than anything else?

3) How are you currently using social media?

Are you scrolling aimlessly? Sharing memories? Seeking likes? Evaluate how you are currently using social media and if you are happy with the way it is being used.

These are only three points to get you started on evaluating how you are connecting via social media platforms. There are so many other questions that we must ask ourselves to ensure that we are utilizing the tools we have been provided to create relationships rather than hinder them.

FAMILY CHAT

Q – During the 2020 quarantine, how have you used social media to stay connected?

Morgan Ortiz (12) – I have still stayed connected with my friends, but I haven't used any social media. Mainly, all my friends have Xbox. I have stayed connected in that way.

Brycen Ortiz (18) – A lot of what I've done is just reach out to people that I haven't talked to in a while. Messaging and reaching out and asking how they have been doing. I've mostly texted them and asked how they have been through everything that's going on. I've let them know that I'm here if they need someone to talk to.

Tate Ortiz (21) – Honestly, the first month I was on social media all the time. But, now I'm back home in Florida and all my college friends are in Tennessee, so I don't get on as much. I didn't want to see all the places they were going without me.

My Family's Quick Guide to Social Media Platforms

TikTok

Dan Ortiz – It's a great place to show your fun side without fear of judgment. I think the quirkier and more fun you are with it, the more celebrated you are on TikTok.

Jennifer Ortiz – I have a love/hate relationship with TikTok. I hate that you can't censor the language. But, I do love it. I took it off of my phone, because I was finding myself losing time. But, I will get on there when I have some time to kill and I stick to the people I follow. I like that they're short.

Makenna Ortiz (23) – TikTok is really funny. A lot of people are involving their parents in it and you can scroll and see a bunch of really creative stuff on there. I love it because it is an amazing platform for people. It's like mini YouTube videos. I admire people's wit and creativity.

The bad, as with any app, is that you can get so consumed by the views and likes. You could have one that goes viral for no reason. So, depending on where your self-esteem is at, you could get consumed in it.

Brycen Ortiz (18) – It is a great app for making people laugh and enjoying. I feel like you should post authentic videos. If you are a funny guy, post funny skits. If you are a dancer, post dances. But, don't take yourself to seriously. Be authentic.

Tate Ortiz (21) – We had vine and it was awesome, but now we have TikTok. I like that they are short. There's a lot of people that wouldn't post a 30-second YouTube video. Little do they know that is all of it and there is nothing else there. It is my favorite social media app right now.

Twitter

Jennifer Ortiz – I don't like Twitter, because it's monitored. It's not true. The things that people tweet are true, but if the monitors of Twitter don't like it, they can remove it. It's not unbiased.

Makenna Ortiz (23) – I had a Twitter account. But, personally, I really didn't understand it. I would overthink things. And, it is a very political app. I really stay out of that stuff, so I didn't find it necessary.

Dan Ortiz – It is like a happy hour cocktail. Gary Vaynerchuck likens it to a networking event. You can pop in and give your opinion on any topic.

Brycen Ortiz (18) – Great app for staying informed. I follow a lot of sports agents. But, it also has a lot of beef and can be a very negative environment as well.

Tate Ortiz (21) – I stay away from that. Twitter is dangerous. How can you describe your entire belief system in 120 characters? The base values of any belief system are just awful. You have a bunch of people talking about their political views and you're like all your opinions look stupid because they are 120 characters.

<u>Facebook</u>

Jennifer Ortiz – Great for businesses. It has changed. It is not what it used to be. I work with teen moms, so I'll use it for a private group. I kind of look at Facebook like my photo album. I'll post to Instagram and share to Facebook. I kind of just do it to keep family and friends up to date.

Makenna Ortiz (23) – I look at Facebook and see how my parents have been able to connect to people they hadn't connected with in a while. My age group uses Instagram. I think it has to do with visuals. We're all about visuals. And, a lot of people use

Facebook to complain. I know that a lot of adults are going to complain and I don't want to see that, so I tend to stay away from Facebook for those reasons.

Dan Ortiz – I view Facebook as digital memories for family and friends. It will be what my great-grandchildren look at to see what 'Pops' was like. A place to connect with old friends. Catching up with old friends. During one of our back-porch talks, we had a little interview segment with people we hadn't seen in 30 years. It was really nice.

Brycen Ortiz (18) – Great for old people.

Tate Ortiz (21) – It's for an older generation. It's best for people that didn't grow up in a social media world. I said earlier, my grandma got on Facebook and we all abandoned it. It's like girls like to post pictures of themselves on the beach, but they don't do that with grandma on there, so maybe that's why we all left and went to Instagram.

Myspace

Jennifer Ortiz – Oh, that's still in existence? I have no opinion.

Makenna Ortiz (23) – (laughing uncontrollably) I never had a Myspace page.

Dan Ortiz – I've been trying to recover that thing and see what I put on it. But, I can't recover it.

Brycen Ortiz (18) – Dead.

Tate Ortiz (21) – I have never been on Myspace and have no idea. I did have a running joke that I was going to make an account so that one day I'd be the only account and it would literally be 'My Space.'

Zoom

Jennifer Ortiz – I like Zoom. I used it for business stuff a lot. But, then when everything happened with Quarantine 2020, I started using it more for personal use, like chatting with family and friends.

Makenna Ortiz (23) – It's interesting, because Skype and Google hangout can do the same thing. But, Zoom has gotten popular.

Dan Ortiz – Zoom has been another great tool to connect with people. With everything that is going on in the world today, I think it has helped accelerate changes in the way we do business by two or three years. Think about this, before I would have had to use an expense account to travel, drive or fly somewhere to meet a potential client. Now, all you have to do is jump on a 'Zoom Call' to achieve the same result. Don't get me wrong, face-to-face interaction in certain moments for business is necessary. But, I would argue that 80% of face-to-face business meetings are not necessary. This tool, called Zoom, will cause companies to rethink how many of their employees are necessary in a brick-and-mortar building versus how many can work from home and get the same or even better production out of teams. I also believe expense accounts for sales people will be cut, because so much of the travel is simply no longer necessary.

Brycen Ortiz (18) – It's something I've used a lot. It is great for classrooms and colleges. My lacrosse team has used it a lot to stay connected. It's an all-around amazing app.

Tate Ortiz (21) – Well, I'm a college student. So, the first time I heard about it was when they told me all my classes would be taken on it. I don't think it's bad. But, I've only had to use it for classes and had problems with it. A lot of times, I'd try talking and it would cut out. It's not very good for educational purposes, in my opinion. I think it's misused for teaching classes.

Instagram

Jennifer Ortiz – I love Instagram. I have bought so much stuff off Instagram, because of the ads that come through it. We live in Florida and the décor is either country or beach. I like farmhouse stuff and followed a lot of farmhouse décor companies. I was able to purchase a lot of stuff that I enjoy. Instagram is great to show off your talents to the world.

Makenna Ortiz (23) – I personally love Instagram, because I feel like it is a personal-picture journal. It's a unique community in its own way. Instagram is a photo blog to me. It can be very easy to get stagnant and say, "Here's a pretty picture of me, like it." It's a way to connect with people and keep up with their lives. It helps you remember that certain people exist.

Dan Ortiz – Instagram is more like a community. It's a cool place to build a community around things that you like. Like with lacrosse. There's an Instagram lacrosse community. Search hashtags and find stuff that you are interested in. A lot of people use these places for search versus Google, because of the visual. I'll search #steak.

Brycen Ortiz (18) – It is a very influential app. A lot of positive influences. But, like with Twitter, it can also get negative.

Tate Ortiz (21) – I think Instagram is the best of Twitter and Facebook. You got the short posts. Most people aren't trying to get political, unless there is something going on. It's the only one that has a wide age-range.

Pinterest

Jennifer Ortiz – I love Pinterest for very specific things. Recipes would be my number one reason and my number two reason would be for holidays. People have thousands of ideas and routines that they have posted. With any social media platforms, you can get sucked in and lose so much time. So, I recommend setting a specific thing that you'll look for and get off.

Makenna Ortiz (23) – It's a pretty Google. I could find the same things on Google. But, Pinterest makes it look really pretty.

Dan Ortiz – I don't use it. I've tried, and I just didn't get it.

Brycen Ortiz (18) – I'm not on Pinterest. From what I've seen from my mom, it's great for gardening.

Tate Ortiz (21) – I've never used it. I hear my mom gets a lot of recipes from it.

Snapchat

Jennifer Ortiz – Snapchat is dangerous, because the pictures go away. So, hurtful or painful things can be sent and there's not much accountability. Makenna and I have cried with laughter over some of the filters, because they are so funny. But, Snapchat really scared me, because there wasn't a real way of keeping up with what the kids were seeing.

Makenna Ortiz (23) – I hate phone calls and don't like calling people I don't know. With Snapchat, you get the satisfaction of seeing someone's face, without FaceTime.

Dan Ortiz – I love using it less and less. I used to use it a lot when Makenna was in college. We would send each other a picture at 4:20 p.m. every day. Not because we're potheads. It was just a funny thing we started. Once Instagram put in their story feature, that moved a lot of people over from Snapchat to Instagram.

Brycen Ortiz (18) – It' great for staying in contact with friends. I would say Snapchat is one of the best apps for keeping in touch with friends.

Tate Ortiz (21) – Snapchat is the Twitter of pictures. It is short, out-of-context pictures all the time. I used to use it a lot. But, I don't anymore. I think it's because I became more normal. I have a group message with some friends and we just post weird stuff. I find a lot of my mischievous friends like to stay on there, because of the 24-hour timeline.

CPSIA information can be obtained
at www.ICGtesting.com
Printed in the USA
FSHW021125220421
80660FS